LAUNCH PAD
LIBRARY

CELEBRATIONS
AND
FESTIVALS

PETER CHRISP

STAMPLEY

How to use this book

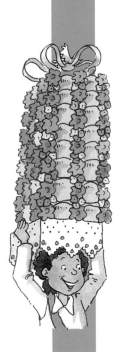

Cross-references
Above some of the chapter titles, you will find a list of other chapters in the book that are related to the topic. Turn to these pages to find out more about each subject.

See for yourself
See-for-yourself bubbles give you the chance to test out some of the ideas in this book. They explain what you will need and what you have to do to see if an idea really works.

Quiz corner
In the quiz corner, you will find a list of questions. The answers to the quiz questions are somewhere in the same chapter. Try to answer all the questions about each subject.

Chatterboxes
Chatterboxes give you interesting facts about other things that are related to the subject.

Glossary
Difficult words are explained in the glossary on page 31. These words are in **bold** type in the book. Look them up in the glossary to find out what they mean.

Index
The index is on page 32. It is a list of important words mentioned in the book, with page numbers next to the entries. If you want to read about a subject, look it up in the index, then turn to the page number given.

Contents

Celebrating!

Celebrations and festivals are important times when people get together to observe significant occasions. Birthday parties and wedding anniversaries celebrate important days in a person's life. The coming of each New Year calls for a celebration. Christmas and Eid-ul-Fitr are marked by religious festivals. Special days are set aside for remembering famous people and past events.

▼ The Festival of Kings in Spain celebrates the Christian story of three wise men who gave gifts to the baby **Jesus**.

▲ At New Year in Myanmar, or Burma, people wash away the old year with water.

Religious festivals
A **religion** is a set of beliefs that affects a person's way of life. **Christianity**, **Judaism**, **Sikhism**, **Islam**, and **Hinduism** are some of the main religions. During festivals, believers celebrate people and events in the history of their religion.

Men dressed as kings throw candy from the back of a large truck.

Fun and games

All over the world, people celebrate in similar ways. They exchange presents, decorate their homes, and share special meals. People may spend weeks or months preparing for important festivals.

The candy reminds people of the gifts that were given to Jesus.

▲ These Canadian-Indian children are at a festival that celebrates their people's history and way of life.

Quiz Corner

● Name two reasons for holding a celebration or festival.

● Where does the Festival of Kings take place?

● How do people in Myanmar celebrate New Year?

Look at: Celebrating, page 4; Fasts and Feasts, page 16

New Year

Around the world, the beginning of a new year is a time for celebration. In many countries, New Year is on January 1, but some religions and countries celebrate it at different times. New Year is often seen as a time to make a fresh start. People follow **customs**, such as cleaning their homes or paying debts, in the hope that good luck will follow.

A new beginning

In China, each New Year falls on a different day, sometime between late January and the middle of February. Each year is named after one of twelve animals, including the monkey, tiger, and pig. In temples, on New Year's Eve, people pray for peace. At home, families hang up red decorations for luck and lock the doors to keep out ghosts. On New Year's Day, millions of firecrackers are exploded in the streets to scare away evil spirits.

▶ At New Year, Chinese people dance through the streets carrying dragons made of cloth or paper.

In Scotland, people believe that you will have good luck if your first visitor of the year is a tall, dark man carrying a lump of coal for the fire. The visitor sometimes brings a drink, too. This custom is called first-footing.

Watching the clock

In towns and cities, people often gather in public squares to hear the clocks strike midnight. After the twelfth chime, people cheer, dance, and sing songs to welcome the new year.

Festive food

In many countries, people eat special food at New Year. Italians make a meal of pigs' feet and lentils, while some Scottish people enjoy a dish of red herring. In southern China, people believe that it is lucky to eat lots of sticky cakes.

SEE FOR YOURSELF

Find out when different religions and countries hold their New Year celebrations. You may need to ask an adult to help you. Mark the dates on a **calendar**.

Quiz Corner

● When does New Year's Day fall in your country?

● Why do Chinese people hang red decorations at New Year?

● What do people carry with them when they go first-footing in Scotland?

Look at: Fasts and Feasts, page 16

Carnival

Carnivals are huge festivities at which people play music, wear colorful costumes, and dance. Carnivals began long ago as a celebration held before Lent, a time when many **Christian** people fast, or stop eating certain foods. Carnivals can include feasting, merrymaking, and masquerades.

▲ This girl is taking part in the Trinidad carnival. Think of all the work it took to make her costume.

Dancing in the streets

One of the biggest carnivals in the world takes place in Rio de Janeiro, Brazil. Many people spend all year designing and making their costumes for the main parade. Musicians play a type of dance music called samba and samba dance schools compete fiercely with choreography, stories and beautiful, fancy costumes. Prizes are given for the best floats, costumes, music and dancing.

SEE FOR YOURSELF

Make a carnival mask by cutting out a shape from thin cardboard to fit across your eyes and nose. Cut out eye holes, then decorate the mask. Glue the mask firmly to a stick.

▲ At the Rio carnival in Brazil, singers and dancers perform on huge floats.

Quiz Corner

- When do Christians sometimes fast?

- Name three countries where carnivals take place.

- What type of music is played at the carnival in Rio de Janeiro?

▲ In Venice, Italy, carnival-goers wear beautiful jeweled costumes and put on masks to hide their faces.

Look at: Carnival, page 8

Spring Festivals

Spring is the time of year when warm weather returns after the cold winter. The first flowers bloom, and birds build nests and lay eggs. Everything seems to burst into activity, so it's a time when people like to celebrate new life and hope for the future.

▶ In Switzerland, people say goodbye to winter and hello to spring by burning a huge model of a snowman.

Holi

Holi is a **Hindu** festival that marks the coming of spring. People celebrate by throwing colored paint at each other. They do this to remember a famous story about their **god** Krishna, who threw colored water all over his friend Radha, the milkmaid. She threw some back and soon the pair were drenched in bright paint.

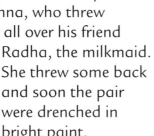

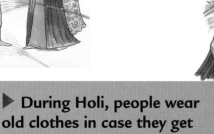

▶ During Holi, people wear old clothes in case they get splattered with paint.

Easter

Christians believe that **Jesus** died on a Friday and that God raised him from the dead three days later. They celebrate this on Easter Day. In many countries, Easter falls in the spring, when sunshine and warmth make plants grow. Flowers are often used in Easter celebrations. They are a reminder of new life.

Eggs at Easter

At Easter, it is the **custom** to give eggs because they stand for new life. They are usually made of candy, but some people give hard-boiled eggs with painted shells.

▲ In Guatemala, people make beautiful carpets from flower petals for the Easter processions.

SEE FOR YOURSELF

To make an Easter egg, blow up a balloon, then cover it with newspaper strips soaked in flour and water. When the paper is dry, pop the balloon with a pin. Paint the egg, then ask an adult to cut it in half. Fill the egg with candy.

Quiz Corner

● At Easter, why do people give eggs as presents?

● What is the name of the Christian festival held in spring?

● Why do Hindus throw colored paint during Holi?

Look at: Fasts and Feasts, page 16

Harvest Time

At harvest time, people gather, or harvest, food that has been planted and grown that season. Everyone celebrates the end of the hard work. They are also happy because they have enough food to last until the next harvest. As you might expect, harvest festivals are a time for eating. Often, there is a large, special meal, with plenty of fresh harvest food.

Thanksgiving

In the United States, the harvest festival is called Thanksgiving. It is held in memory of some English settlers who arrived in North America in 1620. They came in winter and were cold and hungry. In spring, they planted crops. Native Americans showed them how to grow corn and catch fish. After a year had passed, the English had plenty to eat, so they held a feast.

▶ At the first Thanksgiving in 1621, the English invited their Native American friends to share the harvest.

Family gathering

Today, people in the United States hold Thanksgiving every year in November in memory of the first harvest feast. Families enjoy roast turkey, a dish that was eaten at the first Thanksgiving.

People picked wild plums to eat. ....

12

In Tomar, Portugal, there is a harvest celebration called the Festival of Trays. Girls parade through the streets wearing giant hats made from trays. These are piled with loaves of bread and decorated with flowers.

Harvesting fish

Fish are the harvest of rivers and seas, so fishermen have harvest festivals, too. In Argungu, Nigeria, a fishing festival is held every year on the Sokoto River. It is the only time of year when people are allowed to fish there. The festival lasts for three days, and people can catch as many fish as they like.

▲ In Argungu, there are prizes for the best fishermen and the fastest swimmers.

The settlers caught wild turkey, which they roasted over a fire.

Quiz Corner

● What do people celebrate at harvesttime?

● In what year was the first Thanksgiving held?

● What do girls carry on their heads during the Portuguese Festival of Trays?

Look at: Celebrating, page 4

Festive Lights

For many countries the darkest and coldest time of the year is winter. Long ago, people held festivals to remind themselves that the warmth and light of springtime would return soon. Today, people celebrate many important religious festivals during winter. Lights and shining decorations show that beliefs bring light into people's lives.

▶ Evergreen trees keep their leaves all winter. At Christmas, they remind people of life during the winter darkness.

The star reminds people of the star above Jesus' stable.

Christmas

On December 25, Christmas Day, **Christians** celebrate the birth of **Jesus**. They believe that Jesus was born in a stable. A bright star shone over the stable, guiding three wise men and a group of shepherds there. The wise men came from faraway lands and brought rich gifts for Jesus.

bright star

three wise men offer gifts

shepherds

baby Jesus

Guiding lights

Lights are an important part of a **Hindu** festival called Diwali. Hindus light lamps and place them outside their windows and doors to welcome Lakshmi, **goddess** of good fortune. They hope that Lakshmi will bring them prosperity for the coming year.

◀ At Diwali, Hindus light small clay lamps called divas.

Sparkling lights and ornaments, representing faith and hope, decorate the Christmas tree.

People keep presents under the tree until it is time to open them.

CHATTERBOX

In Sweden, there is a beautiful candlelit procession to honor Lucia, the **saint** of light. At the front of the procession, a girl wears a circle of candles set in green leaves on her head. She also carries a tray of sweet buns.

Quiz Corner

● Why do Hindus light lamps during Diwali?

● What do Christians celebrate on December 25?

● Which country has a festival to remember Saint Lucia?

Look at: New Year, page 6; Carnival, page 8

Fasts and Feasts

At certain times of the year, people of many religions eat nothing or very little. This is called fasting. People fast because they believe that by giving up food and feeling hungry, they will become less greedy and less selfish. Some fasts end with a celebration or feast, when everyone has plenty to eat.

Ramadan

The **Muslim** time of fasting lasts one month and is called Ramadan. During this time, Muslims do not eat during daylight hours. They spend many hours reading from the Muslim **holy** book, called the Koran. At the end of the fast, there is a great festival called Eid-ul-Fitr. Everyone wears their best clothes and prays in the mosque. The people are pleased to have kept the long fast of Ramadan.

▲ Muslim families celebrate the end of Ramadan with a feast.

▶ During Eid-ul-Fitr, people give each other cards that say Eid Muburak, which means "Happy Festival."

Yom Kippur

For **Jews**, the most solemn day of the year is Yom Kippur. On this day, in order to show sorrow for the wrong things they have done that year, Jews do not eat or drink. Yom Kippur comes soon after the Jewish New Year and, like other New Year festivals, it is a way of making a fresh start.

▲ The end of the Jewish fast is announced with a blast on the shofar, a trumpet made from a ram's horn.

Quiz Corner

● Why is Yom Kippur a solemn day?

● In what ways do Muslims end the fast of Ramadan?

● Which time in the Christian year is linked to Pancake Day?

Look at: Festive Lights, page 14

Births and Birthdays

The birth of a baby is always a special event. In many religions there is a **ceremony** to name the baby and give it a good start in life. The ceremony welcomes the baby into the family and into the family's religion. Every year, as the baby grows up, friends and family remember his or her birth with a birthday party.

▲ In Great Britain, guards parade through the streets of London to celebrate the Queen's birthday.

Birth and baptism

A **Christian** birth ceremony is called a baptism. It is usually held in a church. During the ceremony, the baby's mother and father promise to teach their child to follow the Christian way of life. Water is sprinkled on the baby and the sign of the cross is made on the baby's forehead.

CHATTERBOX

Sikhs name a new baby by looking in their **holy** book, called the Guru Granth Sahib. The book is opened, and the parents choose a name that begins with the first letter on the left page.

At a Mexican birthday party, children take turns wearing a blindfold. They try to break a papier-mâché animal, called a piñata, with a stick.

Candy and gifts fall out of the broken piñata.

Birthday parties

The day of the year on which you were born is your own special day, your birthday. Often, family and friends mark your birthday by giving you presents and cards. They decorate a birthday cake with candles. When you blow the candles out with one puff, you can make a wish.

Quiz Corner

- How do Sikhs choose names for their babies?

- What promise do parents make at a baptism?

- What is inside a piñata?

Look at: Births and Birthdays, page 18

Growing Up

There are many celebrations for children. In Japan, Children's Day is a fun time for girls and boys of all ages. In **Judaism**, there is a special celebration, called a bar or bat mitzvah, to mark the age at which a child is believed to become an adult.

▶ In Japan on Children's Day, families fly streamers shaped like a type of fish called a carp.

Bar mitzvah and bat mitzvah
In Judaism, a boy of thirteen and a girl of twelve are seen as adults. After a boy's thirteenth birthday, he has a **ceremony** called a bar mitzvah. Before the bar mitzvah, he must study hard to learn Jewish law and a book of **holy** writings called the Torah. These studies will help him to become an adult. There is a similar event for girls, which is called a bat mitzvah.

▶ At his bar mitzvah, a boy reads from the Torah in front of his family and friends.

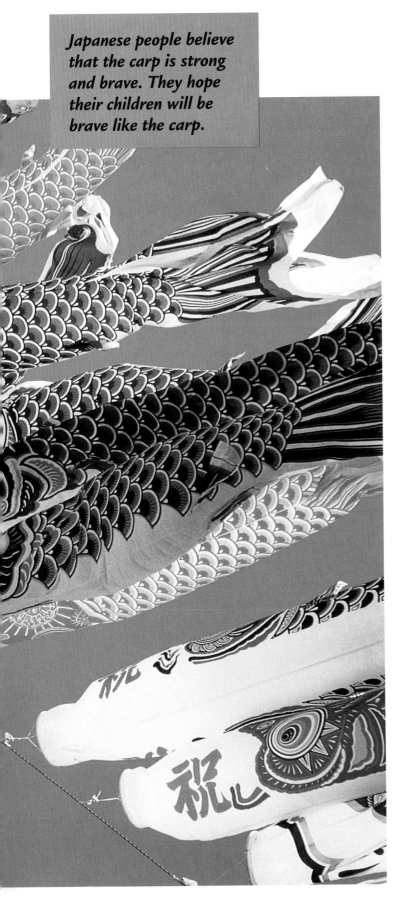

Japanese people believe that the carp is strong and brave. They hope their children will be brave like the carp.

Graduation

When students finish their time at school or college, they are invited to a graduation ceremony. They wear special clothes, such as gowns and square hats, and each student is given a certificate. For many students, leaving school and starting work is an important part of growing up.

Quiz Corner

- At what ages do Jewish children become adults?

- What special clothes do students wear at graduations?

- In Japan, why do families fly streamers shaped like carp?

Marriage

When two people marry, they mark the beginning of a new life together. Most couples are married in a **ceremony** in a public building, such as a church. There, the couple promises to love and care for each other forever. Afterward, there may be a big celebration with food, music, and dancing. The couple receives gifts to help them in their new life.

▼ **Hindu** brides have their hands and feet painted with a dye called henna to make themselves look beautiful.

Dressing for the occasion

The bride and groom usually wear special costumes for their wedding. The costumes are often traditional, which means they are in the same style that has been worn for many years. In **Christian** ceremonies, it is traditional for the bride to wear white. In India, Hindu brides wear a red sari, or long dress, embroidered with gold thread.

CHATTERBOX

The **custom** of a bride and groom exchanging rings is thought to date back to Ancient Rome. The never-ending circle of a ring stands for the idea that the couple will be together forever.

▲ At weddings, guests wear their finest clothes. This Indian boy is dressed in a turban and silk tunic.

Christian weddings

Around the world, Christian couples get married in church. The ceremony is led by a member of the clergy who counsels the couple about their future life together. Friends and family watch the ceremony and join in the celebrations by singing hymns. When the ceremony is finished, the couple leave the church and pose for photographs. It is a custom for the bride to throw her bouquet of flowers to the unmarried, female guests. People say that whoever catches the bouquet will surely be the next to marry.

◀ During the ceremony, passages from the Bible are usually read.

Quiz Corner

- When is the custom of exchanging rings thought to have begun?

- What color dress does a Christian bride wear?

- What is a sari?

# Remembering the Dead

Many countries have festivals to remember people who have died. These festivals are often held in autumn, when the days grow cold and dark. Many of the festivals are happy times, when people show love and respect for their dead relatives by taking flowers to their graves.

SEE FOR YOURSELF

Bobbing for apples is an old Halloween game. To play, fill a bowl with water and float some apples in it. Then, try to pick up an apple with your teeth. Wear old clothes, because you will probably get wet!

CHATTERBOX

In China, at the Festival of Hungry Ghosts, people burn flowers and toy money by the roadsides. These are offerings to people who have died and who have no family to remember them.

▼ Today on Halloween, children dress up in scary costumes and make pumpkin lanterns to put in their windows.

Ghostly fun
Long ago, people in Europe held a festival in autumn, when they believed that ghosts and witches were on the loose. People left out food and drink for them, hoping they would go away. Later, this festival became known as Halloween. It took its name from All Hallows, the **Christian** day for remembering **saints**. Today, Halloween is a fun festival held in Europe and the United States.

▲ On the evening before the Day of the Dead, Mexican families carry vases of colorful flowers down to the graveyards.

Graveyard visitors

On November 2, Mexican people hold a festival called the Day of the Dead. The evening before, people visit graveyards where relatives are buried and picnic there. Many Mexicans stay by the graves all night. The next day is a public holiday, and everyone enjoys a day off work or school. People dress as skeletons and give each other candies shaped like skulls.

Quiz Corner

● When is the Mexican Day of the Dead?

● What do Chinese people burn during the Festival of Hungry Ghosts?

● From where does the name Halloween come?

Sports and Games

All over the world, people love sporting festivals, from school field days to huge events, such as the Olympic Games, that involve hundreds of countries. Many huge events take place in giant stadiums and are watched on television by millions of people all around the world. The celebrations often include **ceremonies**, where the winners receive medals.

▲ Many schools hold field days. Students have time off from classes to take part in games and races.

▲ The winning athlete wears a gold medal; the runners-up wear silver and bronze ones.

The Highland Games

Every year in Scotland, people take part in the Highland Games. The games celebrate Scottish music and dance as well as sports. There are prizes for the best Highland dancer and the best player of a Scottish instrument called the bagpipes.

The Olympic Games

The biggest sporting festival in the world is the Olympic Games, which is divided into the Summer and Winter Games. The games began in ancient Greece in 776 B.C. to honor Zeus, the king of the **gods**. Today, over 65 different kinds of sports are played, from soccer and swimming to gymnastics, bobsledding and horse riding.

▲ This Scotsman is competing in the Highland Games. He is wearing a kilt, a type of skirt that Scottish men wear at special events and celebrations.

▼ At the opening of the Olympic Games in Los Angeles, the crowd held cards to make up the flags of different countries.

Quiz Corner

● Where did the Olympic Games begin?

● Name two contests held at the Highland Games.

● What is a kilt?

Public Holidays

A public holiday is a holiday for everyone in a whole country. Some public holidays celebrate events that led to a country winning independence from foreign rulers. India, Greece, and the United States all have Independence Days. Countries such as Ireland and Mexico have public holidays to honor a particular **saint**, called a patron saint, who is thought to watch over them.

Speeches and games

At many public holidays there are organized celebrations that bring communities together. People hold parades, listen to speeches, and watch games and dances. Everyone has a day off work or school, so that they can join in the celebrations, or even just relax.

▼ On public holidays, children enjoy treats, such as going for a picnic with their family.

▼ Marching bands are popular on Independence Days and Saints' Days.

Bastille Day

The French have a public holiday called Bastille Day. It is held on July 14. On that day in 1789, a large crowd broke into the Bastille prison and freed the prisoners. This was the beginning of the French Revolution, when the people decided that they no longer wanted to be ruled by a king or queen.

the Bastille under attack

◀ Every year in Paris, the storming of the Bastille is celebrated with fireworks.

Quiz Corner

● What was the Bastille?

● Name three countries that celebrate an Independence Day.

● Which days are public holidays in your country?

Amazing Facts

☆ Many Australians eat their Christmas dinner of roast turkey and cranberry sauce on the beach. This is because seasons come at different times in northern and southern parts of the world. In Australia, Christmas Day, or December 25, falls in the middle of summer.

● In Iran, people celebrate New Year on the first day of spring. This festival is called Now Ruz. Families pick fresh rice shoots, tie them with ribbons, and keep them on special tables in their houses. Then, on the thirteenth day of Now Ruz, they go for a picnic and throw the rice shoots into a stream or river.

☆ In Thailand, there is a festival of light known as Loi Krathong. People make little boats, shaped like flowers, out of banana leaves. They take them to rivers and streams, light candles on them, and watch as they drift away. The boats stand for all the unkind thoughts and bad deeds of the previous year, which float away to be forgotten.

● Many Halloween games began as ways of telling the future. After bobbing for apples, people would peel an apple and throw the peel over their left shoulder. The peel was supposed to land in the shape of a letter. This was thought to be the first letter of the name of their future husband or wife.

☆ In Japan, there is a festival in November for girls aged three or seven and boys aged three or five. At this festival, called 3-5-7, children visit a **shrine** where a priest says prayers for each child's future. The children are given candy in bags decorated with turtles and a bird called a crane. These animals stand for long life and good luck.

● Twelfth Night is a festival that began in medieval times and is still celebrated today. It takes place on January 6, the last day of Christmas, when Christians believe the three wise men brought gifts to **Jesus**. In France, a cake is baked for Twelfth Night. Hidden inside is a bean. Whoever has the slice of cake containing the lucky bean becomes "king" or "queen" for the day.

Glossary

calendar A chart that organizes days, months, and years.

ceremony An event or action carried out in a special way to mark an event.

Christianity A **religion** whose members are called **Christians**. They believe that **Jesus** was the Son of God, and they try to follow his teachings.

custom Any act that is repeated over many years.

god/goddess A being who is thought to be more powerful than humans. God is often written with a capital G to show belief in one God.

Hinduism An ancient religion of India whose followers are called **Hindus**. They believe in one God who has many different forms and names, such as Rama and Krishna.

holy A word that describes people, places, animals, or objects that are special to a religion.

Islam A religion whose followers are called **Muslims**. They believe in one God and follow the teaching of their **holy** book, the Koran, which was revealed to the prophet Muhammad. A prophet is someone who is believed to have received a message from God.

Judaism The religion of **Jewish** people. Jews believe in one God and follow teachings from a set of **holy** writings called the Torah.

religion A way of life or set of beliefs that is followed by many people.

saint A **holy** person.

shrine A place where people pray to a **saint** or a **god**.

Sikhism A religion whose followers are called **Sikhs**. They follow a way of life set up by Guru Nanak in north India. They believe in one God, and that all men and women are equal.

Index

Published in the USA by
C.D. Stampley Enterprises, Inc.,
Charlotte, NC, USA.
Created by Two-Can Publishing Ltd.,
London. English language edition
© Two-Can Publishing Ltd, 1997

Art Director: Carole Orbell
Managing Editor: Christine Morley
Senior Commissioning Editor:
Robert Sved
Picture research: Laura Cartwright
Consultant: Mary Hayward
Artwork: Amelia Rosato, Teri Gower,
Mel Pickering
Production: Adam Wilde

ISBN 1-58087-005-8

Photographic credits: front cover:
The Image Bank; p. 4: Robert Harding
Picture Library; p. 5: Britstock IFA; p. 6:
Images Colour Library; p. 8(t): Tony Stone;
(b): Colorific!; p. 9: Superstock; p. 10 (t):
Pictor; (b): Tony Stone; p. 13: The
Hutchison Library; p. 15: Trip; p. 17: Robert
Harding Picture Library; p. 18: Pictor; p. 20
(b): Zefa; pp. 20/21: Britstock IFA; p. 22 (r):
Robert Harding; (l): Rex Features; p. 23:
Tony Stone; p. 25: Tony Stone; p. 26 (l):
Tony Stone; pp. 26/27: Tony Stone; p. 27:
Pictor; p. 28: Pictor; p. 29: Tony Stone.